I0605803

unapologetic

Best Guests Press
9 Broadman Parkway
Jersey City, NJ 07305
201-432-7300
thebestguests.com

Printed in the United States of America.

This book is a compilation of Daniel P. Buttafuoco's responses to Bible and apologetics questions posed by seekers and skeptics of the truth on the Quora platform.

ISBN: 978-0-9973877-6-6

DANIEL P. BUTTAFUOCO

Clear Answers to Tough Bible Questions

A Trial Lawyer's Guide to Winning People, Not Just Arguments

To every believer who loves people enough to seek the truth and speak it with grace.

acknowledgements

This book would not have been possible without the dedication and talent of an extraordinary team.

My deepest gratitude goes to Tom Campisi, whose steady editorial guidance sharpened every page.

Heartfelt thanks to David and Anna Leonard, whose creativity and vision brought the cover design to life in a way that perfectly reflects the spirit of this work.

And to the incredible team at Jungle Communications, Inc., thank you for your unwavering marketing support, tireless energy, and commitment to sharing this project with the world.

Your collective contributions have made this book stronger, brighter, and far more impactful than I could have ever imagined.

foreword

Unapologetic is a timely and urgently needed work by Dan Buttafuoco. As we see God stirring on campuses in the United States, among young people in the UK, and across Asia, this book serves as a powerful resource to help them—and all Christians—engage with their questions about faith.

In Asia alone, we believe one million young people will be challenged to go where the gospel has not yet reached over the next decade. In the UK, church attendance among young men ages 18–24 has risen by 500%. On U.S. campuses, God is moving at places like Ohio State University, where hundreds of baptisms are taking place.

Providing young people with intellectually credible answers to their questions is a lifeline for their faith and witness. On many of our campuses, fewer than 5% of faculty come from an orthodox Christian background, making resources like this invaluable.

I applaud Dan's voice and leadership in apologetics over the decades. His combination of a well-trained mind and a passion for the gospel has proven contagious for committed young people.

I encourage every leader to read this work, study it, and share it with others. Let us join hands to accelerate this important spiritual mission.

Dr. Mac Pier
Founder, Movement.org

preface

When someone asks a tough question about the Bible, you don't need a fierce debate—you need clear and respectful answers. This book is a field guide to help you do exactly that.

Years in courtrooms taught me that clarity, evidence, and care for people matter. The same skills apply when talking about Jesus: the goal is not to win arguments but to serve people with truth—so you can win people, not just arguments.

The questions in these pages were originally posed on Quora by seekers and skeptics from around the world. Each chapter offers direct answers to those questions, presented simply and thoughtfully, to equip you to respond with confidence.

table of contents

What **motivated** first-century Christians to believe and follow Jesus despite risking persecution and even death?

Costly Belief

Why People Ask It

If Christianity were invented, suffering makes no sense. People want to know whether early believers were convinced by truth or carried by myth or pressure.

the case made simple

This question highlights the strongest evidence for the historical reliability of the Christian faith. Unlike some religions—which offered selfish interests (financial and otherwise) to "join" the raiding parties and save your own life by pledging allegiance to a certain religious figure—Christianity spread despite the risks and persecution.

People who do not know history or understand how Christianity started often mistakenly believe that early Christians (a persecuted, marginalized group of powerless people) conspired to make up a good story—one that would potentially get them killed by the Roman authorities: "How about we create a fictional character, call him Jesus, and spin a story that gets him tortured and crucified? Then we will claim that he rose from the dead and that by believing in him you will have eternal life."

Yes, that sounds like a great plan (heavy sarcasm here!). But that's not what happened.

Why would anyone believe this crazy stuff about Jesus in the first-century Roman world unless it was absolutely true? All you got for putting your faith (and belief) in Jesus was persecution from the Jewish leaders and the Roman Empire, an all-powerful government that hated followers of Jesus. Christians were brutally treated. Their property was seized. They were tortured to death, thrown in arenas or used as torches to light Nero's garden. Many fled for their lives, leaving everything behind. There was no earthly reason for becoming a follower of Jesus. It could cost you your life. It often did.

What a great deal! Sign me up.

Nobody wants to believe something that gets you only trouble, violence, and torture. Nobody wants to put their family at risk. Nobody wants to lose everything for which they have worked. And nobody wants to die a painful and excruciating death for something, UNLESS IT'S TRUE.

And early Christians were convinced it was true. They knew what happened. They were present when and where it happened. They spoke to the Apostles. In some cases, they had met Jesus in person, heard him preach, and seen the miracles. And it spread from there. Their motivation came from their conviction that they had seen the risen Jesus and could not deny it, no matter the cost.

What subsequent Christians did immediately afterwards was compile eyewitness testimony about the birth, life, ministry, death, burial, and resurrection of Jesus, THE MOST IMPORTANT PERSON WHO EVER LIVED, if what he claimed was true. If it was false, it was just a harmless superstition. But they spoke to the witnesses. They knew them. The witnesses were credible. They knew the story was fantastic, supernatural, and even strange.

They decided it was true. They were in a position to know for sure. They passed it all on down to us in the form of 27 books which now comprise the New Testament.

We owe a lot to them. They sacrificed their lives and well-being to pass on the truth that Jesus is alive and grants us eternal life. Those writings became the literal foundation for Western Civilization. Those writings contain the Gospel by which we have eternal life.

Paul described these events in 1 Corinthians 15 (verses 1–8):

"Now, brothers and sisters, I want to remind

you of the gospel I preached to you, which you received and on which you have taken your stand. By this gospel you are saved, if you hold firmly to the word I preached to you. Otherwise, you have believed in vain.

For what I received I passed on to you as of first importance: that Christ died for our sins according to the Scriptures, that he was buried, that he was raised on the third day according to the Scriptures, and that he appeared to Cephas, and then to the Twelve. After that, he appeared to more than five hundred of the brothers and sisters at the same time, most of whom are still living, though some have fallen asleep. Then he appeared to James, then to all the apostles, and last of all he appeared to me also, as to one abnormally born."

Thank God for the eyewitness accounts of Christians. They were not liars. They were not fanatics. They were not blind or deaf. They were not insane. They were normal people changed by their encounter with Jesus. They saw the miracles. They saw Jesus crucified. They saw the resurrected Christ.

Closing argument

Early Christians willingly embraced suffering and even death because they were convinced that they had encountered the risen Lord. Their sacrifice stands as powerful evidence that their faith was rooted in TRUTH.

Next steps

Read: 1 Corinthians 15:1–8; Acts 5:27–32

Pray: "Lord, give me clarity and love as I point people to Your resurrection."

How can I know which Old Testament scriptures are still **relevant** when I'm trying to follow New Testament teachings?

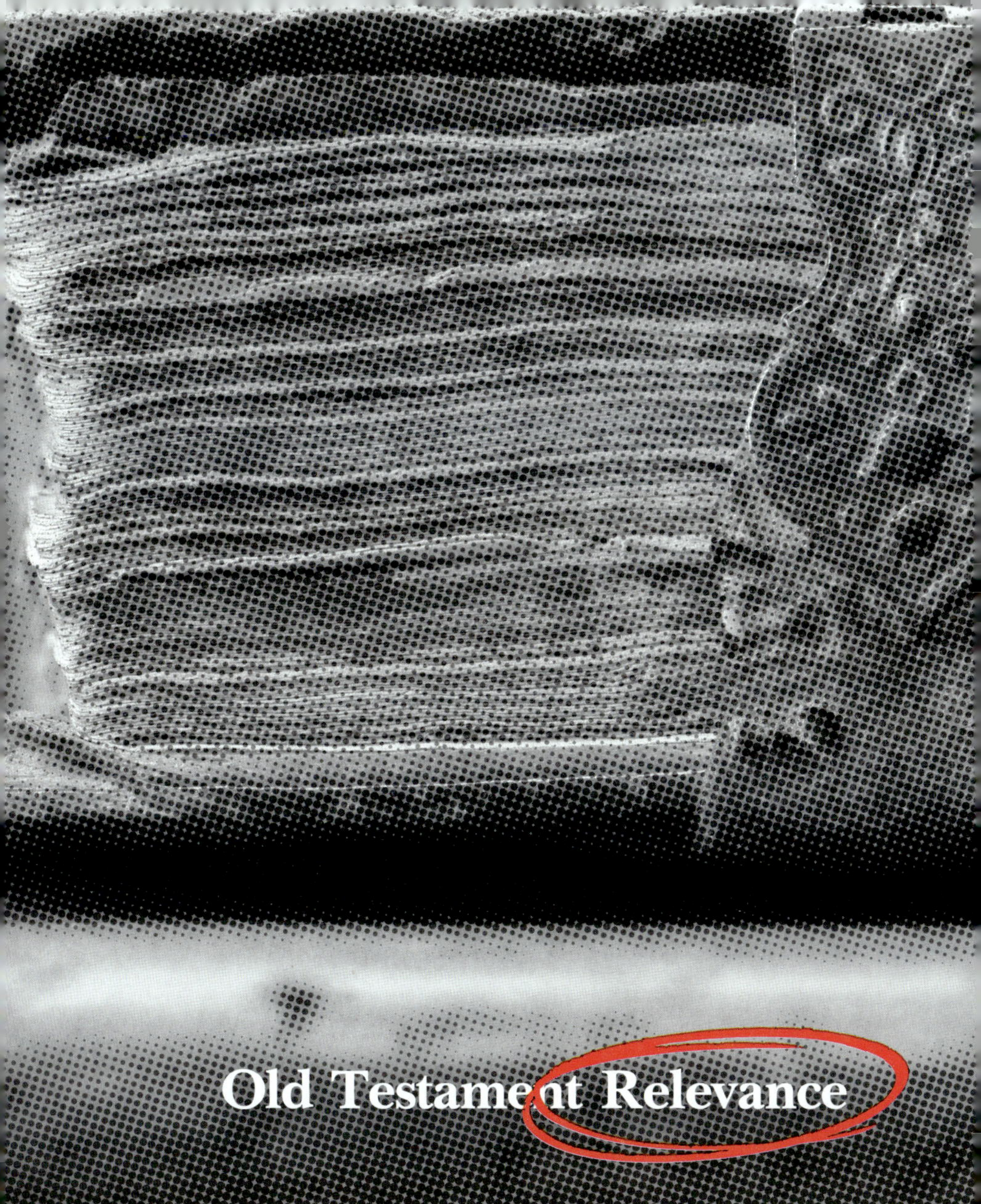

Old Testament Relevance

Why People Ask It

People want to know how the Old Testament—with its laws and ancient practices—is relevant to modern day life.

the case made simple

That is a very good question. One could write a book about it.

Please understand that the entire Bible, including the Tanakh ("Old Testament") is essentially all about Jesus. Always read the Bible with this in mind. Jesus is *"the Word made flesh"* (John 1:14).

Jesus is the living embodiment of the Word of God: *"You search the Scriptures, for in them you think you have eternal life; and these are they which testify of Me."* (John 5:39) He was speaking about the Old Testament (OT).

All Scripture (including the OT) reflects upon, testifies about, and points to Jesus Christ!

Today, we "see" Jesus through the pages of the New Testament, especially in the Gospels. Plus, we have the Holy Spirit "within us" to bear witness to Him.

IS THE OT OBSOLETE?

In speaking about New and Old Testaments, Hebrews 8:13 declares: *"By calling this covenant 'new,' he has made the first one (OT) obsolete; and what is obsolete and growing old will soon disappear."*

The Book of Hebrews is generally dated to the period between 60 and 70 AD. This book talks in detail about the elaborate sacrificial system in place at the Temple in Jerusalem. The writer communicates the sacred importance of the altar, with the priests and Levites all performing daily sacrifices.

Jesus predicted the end of this age (Matthew 24:3, Luke 21). This happened in 70 AD. The Romans destroyed the Temple. It is a recorded fact of history. As Jesus prophesied, *"not one stone would be left upon another."*

The Old Covenant (OT) became obsolete. Even Jews today no longer practice animal sacrifices.

WHY KEEP THE OLD TESTAMENT?

If the Old Covenant is obsolete, why is the OT still in Christian Bibles?

Jesus explains in Matthew 5:

> *"Do not think that I have come to abolish the Law or the Prophets; I have not come to abolish them but to fulfill them."*

In Jewish tradition, the Hebrew Bible (also known as the Tanakh) is divided into three parts: the Law (Torah), the Prophets (Nevi'im), and the Writings (Ketuvim).

Jesus **FULFILLED** the first two parts, keeping the Law perfectly and living a sinless life. The third part, the Writings (books like Proverbs and Ecclesiastes) contain timeless wisdom. That was not "fulfilled" because it did not need to be. It still works well. It still applies.

Jesus' last words while dying on that cross were *"IT IS FINISHED"* (John 19:30). Tetelestai (τετέλεσται) is the Greek word used here meaning "it is finished" or it is "paid in full." The word carries a sense of completion, accomplishment, and finality.

All prophecy, law, and foreshadowing of the Messiah were fulfilled.

So, why is the OT still in the Christian Bible? The main reason is for history and context. We need to understand

that Jesus fulfilled the prophecies and the Law. We need the context of life before Christ to understand life after Christ.

THE OLD TESTAMENT'S BRUTALITY

The Old Testament helps us understand the plague of sin. People were exceedingly wicked. They were engaged in constant warfare. They sacrificed their children on burning altars. They practiced slavery. Rape and incest were common.

One cannot fully appreciate what Christ accomplished/finished for us until you know and understand the predicament we were in. The problem of sin and separation from God was, and still is, the issue. That is why you need to read the OT. It will help you appreciate the work of Christ. You cannot appreciate being "saved" until you understand how lost you were.

THE GREATEST COMMANDMENTS

Jesus said the whole law could be summed up in only two commandments: Love God and love people.

Hearing that Jesus had silenced the Sadducees, the Pharisees got together. One of them, an expert in the law, tested him with this question: *"Teacher, which is the greatest commandment in the Law"?*

Jesus replied: *"'Love the Lord your God with all your heart and with all your soul and with all your mind.' This is the first and greatest commandment. And the second is like it: 'Love your neighbor as yourself.' All the Law and the Prophets hang on these two commandments."* —Matthew 22:37–40

LOVE fulfills the law. If you love someone, you will not commit adultery by sleeping with his wife; you will not murder; you will honor your parents; you will not steal. You will be generous; you will be faithful to your spouse. It all falls into place.

You can eat shellfish, you do not have to sacrifice animals, all foods are declared clean, and you will not be damned because of your sin. Do not worry about the written code. God has written the law on your heart! The Spirit is within you, guiding you, showing you what is right and good and holy.

Tetelestai!

Closing argument

The Old Testament is not irrelevant. It is fulfilled.

Next steps

Read: Matthew 5:17–18; Luke 24:27; Hebrews 8:13

Pray: "Jesus, help me read the whole Bible through the lens of Your fulfillment."

How do historians determine which parts of the Gospels contain **historical truth** despite apparent contradictions?

Gospel "Contradictions"

Why People Ask It

Alleged contradictions in the Bible are often highlighted by critics to cast doubt on its reliability.

the case made simple

The Oxford Learner's Dictionary defines contradiction as "a lack of agreement between facts, opinions, actions, etc."

A contradiction, properly defined, DOES NOT EXIST BETWEEN THE GOSPELS.

A contradiction means that they (the different accounts) cannot both be true without reconciling the differences.

As such, there are ZERO CONTRADICTIONS in the GOSPELS. Are there differing accounts of the same story? Without a doubt, yes! But that's not a contradiction. Both accounts can be true. They read the same as any eyewitness testimony. Some witnessed events and reported them and not others. Some recalled some things and reported them and not others.

Only a very simple mind would see that as a contradiction. It is actually a mark of authenticity. These writers did not collude together. They were independent of each other. It's the reason why we exclude witnesses from a courtroom. We don't let them hear or see the other witnesses until after they testify. We don't want people tailoring their stories.

Some saw one angel at the tomb. Another writer saw two. They had different vantage points. It's the way trials are won.

Augustine, one of the most influential early Christian theologians, maintained that if an apparent contradiction was found in Scripture, the error lay with the reader, not the text:

> "If we are perplexed by anything in Scripture, we must be careful not to say, 'The author of this book is mistaken.' Rather, either the manuscript is faulty, or the translation is wrong, or you have not understood it."

In his book, *When Critics Ask: A Popular Handbook on Bible Difficulties*, twentieth-century theologian Norman Geisler made this powerful observation: "Contradictions are the most common allegation made by skeptics against the Bible. Yet no one has ever been able to prove a real contradiction in it. Alleged contradictions usually evaporate upon careful examination of the context and the meaning of the words."

While it is true that there are difficulties in the Bible, the existence of difficulties does not cash out to errors or contradictions, nor is the Christian's inability to answer difficulties or apparent contradictions an admission that the Bible does in fact contain such deficiencies.

All the Christian needs to do is demonstrate that an apparent conflict or contradiction is not in fact a genuine violation of the laws of logic. At this point, the mere existence of a possible reconciliation of two apparently contradictory passages of Scripture demonstrates conclusively that the two are not actual contradictions.

Contrary to what the skeptics say, the modern Bible has only become a more accurate representation of the original as more ancient manuscript discoveries have come to light. Today, we know what the original words are to the highest degree of accuracy.

Closing argument

The critics are misinformed. We have great evidence for the reliability of the texts of the Bible, and that is especially true of the New Testament. Read it with confidence.

Next steps

Read: Luke 1:1–4; John 20; Matthew 28

Pray: "God, make my answers patient, precise, and people-first."

Does the possible existence of the "Q Document" challenge or support belief in the inspiration of the Gospels?

The "Q" Source

Why People Ask It

People want to know if "Q" is a smoking gun or merely a scholarly hypothesis in relation to the Synoptic Gospels.

the case made simple

Matthew, Mark, Luke, and John each wrote accounts of the life, ministry, miracles, and resurrection of Jesus. There are many speculations and theories regarding exactly how the four Gospels were written.

There was, without doubt, a strong oral tradition circulating for about twenty years after the events regarding Jesus of Nazareth, whom many believed to be the Messiah. Witnesses were still living. We know this because—by the time Paul wrote and referenced the *"five hundred witnesses, most of whom are still alive"* (1 Corinthians 15:6)—the

Gospels were likely already completed. If the witnesses were still alive you can bet that they were constantly repeating the story and verifying the facts of the amazing events they had observed.

The Hebrew culture, especially the one in which the events surrounding Jesus unfolded, was particularly adept at preserving history and facts using constant repetition. This was a time when people had large portions of the Scripture (and other things) committed to memory. They would have had verbal transmission of amazing stories of a prophet doing miracles, challenging the religious leaders, and rising from the dead.

Scholars believe that before the four Gospels were written, there may have been a document called “Q” that recorded an account of the teachings and ministry of Jesus (“Q” is from the German word Quelle, meaning “source”). We do not have a copy of that account, if it even existed. It is a theory based on the way the four Gospels (Matthew, Mark, Luke, and John) were written and the fact that the first three (called the “Synoptic Gospels”) share certain characteristics in grammar, wording, and material that appear to make them related to a common source. It is also possible that one of them (the Gospel of Mark, the earliest) was used as that source and “Q” never existed at all. We don’t know one way or the other.

The existence or non-existence of “Q” has utterly no

bearing on the issue of Divine inspiration. It's just a theory, regardless.

The idea here is that the Synoptic Gospel writers (Matthew, Mark, and Luke) might have used this source as a "checklist" reminder to create their own independent eyewitness accounts. Mark wrote Peter's account; Matthew wrote his own account; and Luke interviewed many eyewitnesses such as the Apostles, the family members of Jesus, Mary (Jesus' mother), and whoever else had relevant testimony regarding Jesus.

God watched over his Word. He presented it and preserved it exactly as he intended.

God uses the talents, faculties, and intellect of his people, particularly in this endeavor of great importance. The fact that they may have referred to an outline to refresh their memories or to prompt an account is a good thing. It's like using notes as a reminder to create a more flowing and readable account which ultimately became the Gospels. We use such tools when we do public speaking in court or in church.

Tatian, writing in the second century, tried to harmonize the four Gospels into a single work (four into one) called the Diatessaron. It was widely used by the Syriac Church. That was the reverse of the "Q" theory (one into four).

The point is that, as Luke notes in the opening sentence

of his Gospel, "many have undertaken to write down these things." This implies that there was much more in the way of written material that was documented by the followers of Jesus. That should come as no surprise. It was big news!

I have no problem with Q. In fact, I would love it if a copy turned up. You never know.

Closing argument

The possible existence of Q does not preclude divine inspiration.

Next steps

Read: Matthew 5:17–18; Luke 24:27; Hebrews 8:13

Pray: "Jesus, help me read the whole Bible through the lens of Your fulfillment."

What do you think about Jesus Christ? **Is He real** or just a myth?

Jesus

Why People Ask It

People ask if Jesus is real because they are seeking evidence to determine whether He was truly the Son of God or simply a legendary figure, like those found in Greek mythology.

the case made simple

It is very clear what Jesus did, what he said, and who he is. All you need to do is read the New Testament.

If you want FACTS about Jesus, simply read the eyewitness accounts. You do not have to guess or speculate:

> *"Many have undertaken to draw up an account of the things that have been fulfilled among us, just as they were handed down to us by those who from the first were eyewitnesses and servants of the word.*

Since I myself have carefully investigated everything from the beginning, I too decided to write an orderly account for you, most excellent Theophilus, so that you may know the certainty of the things you have been taught."—Luke 1:1–3

Here are a few other compelling eyewitness accounts:

"For we did not follow cleverly devised stories when we told you about the coming of our Lord Jesus Christ in power, but we were eyewitnesses of his majesty."—2 Peter 1:16

"That which was from the beginning, which we have heard, which we have seen with our eyes, which we have looked at and our hands have touched—this we proclaim concerning the Word of life. The life appeared; we have seen it and testify to it, and we proclaim to you the eternal life, which was with the Father and has appeared to us. We proclaim to you what we have seen and heard, so that you also may have fellowship with us. And our fellowship is with the Father and with his Son, Jesus Christ. We write this to make our joy complete."—1 John 1:1–4

"Then they called them in again and commanded them not to speak or teach at all in the name of Jesus. But Peter and John replied, 'Which is right in God's

eyes: to listen to you, or to him? You be the judges! As for us, we cannot help speaking about what we have seen and heard.'"—Acts 4:18–20

As a trial lawyer, I take any testimony or eyewitness account for what it is worth based on the credibility of the persons testifying. If the testimony is overwhelming, consistent with time, space, geography and other witnesses in the major points, and UNOPPOSED (by that I mean, that there is no contrary testimony), then I believe it.

And early Christian witnesses were cross-examined, as well. They were cross-examined by torture, and many were put to death. Many of them died horrible deaths after being inflicted with the worst tortures. I find this extremely credible; this is probably why God allowed it to happen. Nobody recanted. All went to their martyrdom proclaiming, "Jesus rose from the dead!"

I have seen witnesses unravel after a few short questions on cross-examination. That level of discomfort does not begin to compare with what the New Testament witnesses had to endure.

That unwavering testimony, sealed in blood, is the strongest evidence that their proclamation, "Jesus rose from the dead," was the truth.

Closing argument

The New Testament contains numerous eyewitness accounts. They make a strong case for the life, death, and resurrection of Jesus Christ.

Next steps

Read: Luke 1:1–4; 2 Peter 1:16; 1 John 1:1–43

Pray: "Jesus, reveal Yourself to seekers and make my words gracious."

How do ancient manuscript **errors and translations** impact how we understand the New Testament?

Manuscripts and Variants

Why People Ask It

They often ask this because differences in ancient manuscripts and translations can raise questions about the accuracy and reliability of the New Testament.

the case made simple

They don't impact the message of the New Testament at all.

Christians who love Jesus believe in the doctrine of "plenary inspiration" and inerrancy of the Scripture.

What that means is that we believe (based on a whole host of factors) that the Bible is the Word of God. It was written by men of God "moved by the Holy Spirit." In the ORIGINAL WRITINGS (the "autographa") there were absolutely no errors. We believe it is the absolute truth, grounded in history and without any error.

Here's where it gets dicey. There is no doubt that, over the centuries, when the text was copied there were errors introduced into the text by various scribes. While some early scribes were professional and exact in how they copied the 27 books of the New Testament, some others were, frankly, sloppy amateurs.

The result? We have thousands of little variants in the text which lead critics of the Bible to doubt the validity of the text. Were the writings of the New Testament accurately preserved? This is a valid question.

There's much written on this topic, but I'll make it simple.

The Bible is the most widely copied and translated book in the world and the bestseller year after year. Because the New Testament was copied so many times by so many people and has had so many translations over the years, we know with great accuracy what copyist errors were made and can easily identify them.

Additionally, there are so many ancient manuscripts (over 27,000; I have some of them) that it's easy to compare the various copies and ascertain where a scribe skipped a line, left out a word, inserted a pronoun, added punctuation, or his own theological commentary. And that's what we are talking about. Most of these so-called "variants" are unimportant and don't change the meaning of the text at all.

The result? We know almost exactly what the original writers of the New Testament wrote. This was done before we had computers. Now, with computers, it's very easy to cross-reference all important texts and spot and correct the variants.

With the consistent discovery of older and more reliable manuscripts over the last two hundred years, we now know that there are only about 40 lines of the New Testament in dispute. And none of them affects a teaching of Christ or an important doctrine of the Christian faith. NONE!

It is really all a big non-issue, the fodder of nit-picking Bible critics. I guarantee you that the average person would not recognize any significant difference in the texts from one translation to the other.

As an example, let's look at the King James Bible (KJV), which was published in 1611. I have an original in my collection because I am a Bible nerd and a committed follower of Jesus who is interested in this stuff. In the King James Bible, the text of the New Testament was based on the "Textus Receptus" (Latin for "received text"). This text was the THIRD edition of a printing of the New Testament (I also have a copy of that) by Robertus Stephanus. It was based on the groundbreaking work of Erasmus of Rotterdam, a towering biblical scholar and intellectual who published the first printed edition of the Greek New Testament. I also have that original book.

The problem? Erasmus only had seven or eight manuscripts in his possession. Despite that reality, we got a very accurate version of the New Testament that was incorporated into the King James Version. The translators used that book at Hampton Court to produce the KJV in 1611.

Today, we now have available about 27,000 manuscripts. With the help of computers and biblical scholarly giants like Nestle and Aland, we have a much more accurate text! You can easily verify all of this with a little research.

The bottom line: you can read your Bible with confidence! More work has gone into producing an accurate New Testament than you can possibly imagine. We have the words of Jesus and the Apostles! Your faith is secure.

So, when you hear so-called scholars writing books like Misquoting Jesus (Bart Ehrman), understand that they have an agenda to make money and are only sensationalizing what Bible scholars have known for centuries, namely that copyists made errors when they copied the text by hand.

If I asked you to copy the entire New Testament, you would also make some errors. So would everyone who copied it. But since it was copied by so many people at so many times and places, and in so many languages, everyone made different errors.

We have the Bible! It's accurate. Don't shy away from the truth. If someone tells you there were copyist errors in the

Bible, tell them, "So what? WE HAVE RECLAIMED THE ORIGINAL TEXT WITH GREAT ACCURACY."

The modern translations recognize this and are, therefore, the most accurate. But you can get saved, born again and become a solid Christian even with the King James version, despite its minor problems.

You only need one verse: John 3:16, *"For God so loved the world that he gave his one and only Son, that whoever believes in him shall not perish but have eternal life."* That verse, like many others, is not in dispute!

Closing argument

While ancient scribes made small mistakes in copying, these errors and translations don't impact how we understand the New Testament. The message of God's Word remains intact, and trustworthy, preserved with accuracy across centuries.

Next steps

Read: 2 Timothy 3:16; Luke 1:1–4

Pray: "God, thank You for preserving Your Word. Help me read it, trust it, and live it."

What are the differences between reading the **New Testament in Greek** and reading it in English as translated in **Jerome's Latin Vulgate** or in the **King James Version?** Which translation is considered more accurate, and why?

Translations

Why People Ask It

With so many Bible study tools and translations available today, committed Christians seek to make sure they are using the most reliable resources.

the case made simple

The differences are related to what best communicates to YOU as the reader. Do you read or speak Greek? If not, then I suggest you find a Bible in your own understandable language.

Which is more accurate? The Greek, of course. But if you cannot understand Koine Greek (the original language of the New Testament), what difference does it make? You would be better off looking at an illustrated children's Bible than a highly accurate Greek one that you cannot read. The same is true of Latin or any other language that you do not read. Read what you can grasp.

In fact, that is exactly how the Church handled it in the Middle Ages when the peasants were largely illiterate. They had artwork everywhere in the churches so that people could visualize the Bible stories in stained glass panels or in paintings and sculptures. The priests and teachers explained the rest. Even pictures can, to a certain extent, transmit truth.

My point here is that it only matters to the extent you can understand it.

Now, if you are asking what Bible is most accurate according to textual critics and scholars, that is an entirely different question.

There are essentially two main lines of text for the New Testament, the Critical Text (earliest and best manuscripts) and the Majority Text (the largest number of manuscripts, but mostly all Byzantine and much later).

Both are good. Both contain truth. Both contain the teachings of Jesus, the words of the Apostles, and the doctrines of the Church. You can be a Christian and read any number of translations. The Bible is the most translated book in the history of the world (for good reason), and it is in just about every known language, including Braille.

They all say the same thing in a different way. They say it in every language. They say it based on different manuscripts.

They say it using different translation methodologies (idiomatic or literal). I think there is even a Bible in Ebonics (a vernacular form of the Bible in African American English). The Word of God is out there everywhere and for everyone.

Regarding the basis for ALL these Bibles and the ancient manuscripts used to translate them, I guarantee you that the average person would not even be able to distinguish either of these from the other without reading and studying the Bible from cover to cover over many months and carefully comparing the two main manuscript families (and their resultant translations). This is the domain of Bible scholars and Bible nerds. If you are a sincere Christian, but not a Bible scholar, you need not concern yourself with these matters. Indeed, most pastors have no idea what I am talking about here. Just pick a translation that suits you and start reading it.

Having said that, the most accurate Bible today is based on the Critical Text.

The King James Bible (KJV), though highly accurate and a very neutral translation, is based on a handful of ancient manuscripts (only seven or eight available to Erasmus). It was translated in 1611 (not by King James but under his direction by a group of the best English scholars). Unless you speak Shakespearean English, it is probably not the best translation for you.

Closing argument

The NIV is based on the Critical Text and is very accurate. That is my preferred Bible (although I still love the poetic sound and majesty of the KJV).

Next steps

Read: Psalm 119:105; John 20:31

Pray: "Lord, lead me to read, understand, and obey Your Word."

What are the reasons for people believing in only one holy book?

The Bible

Why People Ask It

While treating all religious texts as equal may seem humble, it raises the question of whether only one can ultimately be true.

the case made simple

There is one reason and ONE REASON ONLY to believe anything, especially about God. And that one reason is this: Is it true?

Is your "holy book" accurate, true, and factual? Does it comport with reality? Is it historically accurate?

The New Testament was written by eyewitnesses. It is firmly grounded on fact. These people were there. They saw with their own eyes that which they wrote about. Some died for that testimony. They weren't coerced into believing it.

They had no reasons for believing it other than the fact that it was true.

As the Apostle Peter wrote:

> *"For we did not follow cunningly devised fables, when we made known unto you the power and coming of our Lord Jesus Christ, but we were eyewitnesses of his majesty."*—2 Peter 1:16 (ASV)

He first denied Jesus in the face of danger. Later he was martyred for his faith.

Or consider the words of John the Apostle, a member of Christ's inner circle:

> *"That which was from the beginning, which we have heard, which we have seen with our eyes, which we have looked at and our hands have touched—this we proclaim concerning the Word of life."—1 John 1:1*

Or Luke, who wrote a commissioned report to a high-ranking Roman official about Jesus and the faith sweeping throughout the Roman Empire:

Forasmuch as many have taken in hand to set forth in order a declaration of those things which are most surely believed among us,

Even as they delivered them unto us, which from the

beginning were eyewitnesses, and ministers of the word;

It seemed good to me also, having had perfect understanding of all things from the very first, to write unto thee in order, most excellent Theophilus,

> *"That thou mightest know the certainty of those things, wherein thou hast been instructed."*
> —Luke 1:1–4 (KJV)

Luke was reporting so that his patron might know *"The certainty of the things"* he had been told.

It is all about knowing and believing the truth.

Is your religion, your belief system true? Have you investigated it? You should.

We believe in Jesus, Christianity, and the New Testament because it is true. That is the ONLY reason I believe it.

Have you ever heard of Sir William Mitchell Ramsay? If not, you should. He was one of the most respected archaeologists of his time. He was knighted for his accomplishments. He was not exactly a dumb guy.

Ramsay was initially convinced the New Testament—especially the Book of Acts—was unreliable. Just another ancient religious text full of myths and exaggerations. He did what most critics don't: he thoroughly investigated.

He spent 25 years trekking across Asia Minor, mapping ancient cities, examining ruins, and lining up Luke's details

with what the dirt had to say. Ramsay's goal? Expose the errors. The result? He found none.

Time after time, Luke was right. Names, dates, geography, local politics—the kind of details that should've been lost to time—were nailed with precision. Ramsay had to admit it: Luke wasn't just writing inspirational content. He was recording history.

"After 25 years of work and research, traveling Asia and the Middle East, Ramsay was awestruck by the historical accuracy and evidence of the New Testament," writes Al Christie on Substack. "In his quest to refute the Bible, Ramsay discovered many facts which confirmed its precision."

Ramsay finally laid it all out in St. Paul: The Traveller and the Roman Citizen— not as a preacher, but as a scholar. The man who set out to dismantle the credibility of the Bible ended up calling Luke one of the most trustworthy historians of the ancient world.

His conclusion? The Bible holds up. Even under a microscope.

How about Simon Greenleaf, Dean of Harvard Law School and Professor of Evidence?

In 1846, Greenleaf wrote a legal treatise entitled, An Examination of the Testimony of the Four Evangelists by the Rules of Evidence Administered in the Courts of Justice. The short book was an apologetic work written from a

Christian perspective. Greenleaf argued that the eyewitness accounts of the Gospels would stand up under the rules of legal evidence.

Together, the meticulous historical research of Sir William Ramsay and the rigorous legal analysis of Simon Greenleaf converge on the same point: the New Testament is credible. Its events are TRUE.

Closing argument

There is more than enough evidence to prove the resurrection of Jesus Christ. The Bible stands alone as THE source of all truth.

Next steps

Read: John 14:6; Luke 1:1–4

Pray: "God, let truth be compelling and love be evident in my words."

How **reliable are the Gospels** as historical documents in proving the existence of Jesus?

Gospel Reliability

Why People Ask It

People ask this because they are seeking a solid historical foundation and tangible evidence for the life and existence of Jesus.

the case made simple

The Gospels were written by eyewitnesses to the life, ministry, miracles, death, burial, and resurrection of Jesus Christ.

Eyewitness testimony is the same whether it is used today or two thousand years ago. If you haven't already noticed this, some people are better at speaking and communicating than others. Some have very rich vocabularies (and speak multiple languages) while others speak poorly (with limited words) and use grunts and hand signals to try to communicate. They can barely tell a story.

Modern people are increasingly less able to communicate with language clearly and intelligently than in times past and often rely on memes, technology, and media to make their points. Today, people have more information but depend less on their brains. Most cannot even memorize a single phone number (again, relying on their phones to store numbers).

The ancient world was not like that. They had a rich oral tradition in which entire books were memorized by people. Today, people have their heads buried in their phones and barely notice what is happening around them. They text while driving and end up plowing into stopped cars at red lights. I know. I make a nice living representing the people they injure. It is an epidemic.

This decline in focus highlights a key difference between our culture and the ancient one. While we are often careless with observation and memory, people in the ancient world trained themselves to remember and recount what they saw with great care. That is why the question is not whether they experienced real events, but how those experiences were recorded and preserved for us to evaluate.

Nowadays, we can easily video record eyewitness testimony in court. Yet, we still (mostly) do not use it because it is expensive and basically not that important. It is sometimes used in really media famous cases (think the OJ trial) in other states like California. In the average case, even the largest and most important ones, it is not used at all. In New York (hardly a primitive state) it is rarely used. Cameras are not even allowed into the courtroom.

As testimony occurs, the testimony is recorded in real time during the trial by an official court stenographer (i.e. "court reporter") who is trained to work on a stenographic machine to record the testimony. On appeals, we rely on the official court record, which is that transcribed document based on a bunch of symbols that were typed into a stenographic machine. It works quite well. It has been done this way for decades.

Previously, we had trained court reporters who used "shorthand" to record testimony. Years ago, I had an entire trial in which an older court reporter used such a method. He basically was writing script down in shorthand the way my mother used to do as a secretary. The problem could arise if he/she were to die or become disabled as it was hard to find someone who could read that person's own brand/style of notes. Yet, this was how testimony is preserved.

Appellate judges decide million and even billion-dollar cases based on a written court record before them. They don't have video. They have only words that documented eyewitness testimony.

It was not much different in the ancient world. They certainly didn't have videos. They were as accurate as they could be. They wanted to be precise, especially if the topic was of some importance and they knew that they were writing for posterity.

How can we tell which parts of the New Testament were written by eyewitnesses? Well, to begin, some of those texts say that the authors were themselves eyewitnesses to what they were writing about. That was common.

Here are some examples from the New Testament (written 2,000 years ago):

> *"The Word became flesh and made his dwelling among us. We have seen his glory, the glory of the one and only Son, who came from the Father, full of grace and truth."*—John 1:14

> *"For we did not follow cleverly devised stories when we told you about the coming of our Lord Jesus Christ in power, but we were eyewitnesses of his majesty."*—2 Peter 1:16

> *"When they saw the courage of Peter and John and realized that they were unschooled, ordinary men, they were astonished, and they took note that these men had been with Jesus...Then they called them in again and commanded them not to speak or teach at*

all in the name of Jesus. But Peter and John replied, 'Which is right in God's eyes: to listen to you, or to him? You be the judges! As for us, we cannot help speaking about what we have seen and heard.'"
—Acts 4:13, 18–20

Acts 28 demonstrates that the writer (Luke) was PRESENT when the events happened (the use of the pronouns "we" and "us" indicate this):

> *"Once safely on shore, we found out that the island was called Malta. The islanders showed us unusual kindness. They built a fire and welcomed us all because it was raining and cold..." (verses 1–2).*

Of course, these Bible verses are only a small sampling of the numerous eyewitness accounts in Scripture. In a courtroom, judges and juries regularly rely on eyewitness testimony to establish the truth of events. Verdicts are handed down based on what credible witnesses have seen and reported. The same principle holds true with Scripture.

Closing argument

The eyewitness testimonies of the apostles and early disciples, written down and preserved, stand as valid testimony for proving the existence of Jesus.

Next steps

Read: Luke 1:1–4; John 21:24; Acts 27–28

Pray: "Lord, use trustworthy testimony to lead people to You."

How do Christians interpret **Biblical warnings** about **opposition and debates** with non-believers in today's context?

Opposition and Debate

Why People Ask It

Committed Christians want to share their faith and "speak the truth in love," while remaining faithful to biblical teaching.

the case made simple

The Bible says (Jude 3) that we believers are to *"contend for the faith once and for all entrusted to the saints."* That is clear. It's an admonition to all believers to take on the lies of the culture with truth. It means we should oppose, at every turn, those who raise false objections to the Bible, the Gospel, the life and character of Jesus, and the testimony of the Apostles. There are those here on Quora and in society who have absolutely no idea what they are talking about, yet they confidently spread lies concerning the Christian faith. This must be addressed. Every Christian should take this seriously. Every Christian should speak up.

The Apostle Paul wrote that we are to *"demolish arguments and every pretension that sets itself up against the knowledge of God"* (2 Corinthians 10:5). That's for good reason. Lives and souls are at stake. We "demolish" the lies and arguments of the enemy with facts, evidence, logic, and information that is true.

The "devil is a liar," Jesus said. The only way to combat a lie is with the truth. Jesus said, "You shall know the truth and the truth shall make you free."

Every Christian needs to be an apologist. Every Christian should know basic arguments and points for WHY WE BELIEVE WHAT WE BELIEVE.

There are actually very good reasons for believing the truth of the Gospel. A century ago, these things were well known by virtually all educated believers. Today, people go on feelings or their "personal testimony." While there's nothing wrong with sharing your own testimony, you should also know the objective, historical, and evidential reasons for believing the narrative of the New Testament. Be able to explain why you believe in Christ.

The prophecies fulfilled, the corroboration with secular sources, the geographical/cultural accuracy of the accounts, the power of recorded EYEWITNESS testimony, the beauty of the teachings of our Lord, the way the Scriptures were recorded and preserved—these and many other reasons all point to the veracity and truth of the Gospel.

The Apostle Peter said, *"Always be ready to give a reason for the hope that is within you"* (1 Peter 3:15). The Greek word for "reason" is apologia, from which we get the word "apologist" and "apologetics."

There is no excuse for a Christian not to be able to bear witness to the truth against people who raise baseless objections.

Closing argument

As a Christian, you must always be ready to share the precious hope you have in Christ— and be UNAPOLOGETIC in defending your faith.

Next steps

Read: 1 Peter 3:15; 2 Corinthians 10:5; Colossians 4:5–6

Pray: "Jesus, make my words true, my tone gentle, and my love genuine."

Further Readings

to help you always be prepared to give an answer
to everyone who asks you to give the reason for
the hope that you have 1 Peter 3:15

The Case for Christ
Lee Strobel

Can We Trust the Gospels?
Peter J. Williams

The Historical Reliability of the Gospels
Craig Blomberg

Jesus and the Eyewitnesses
Richard Bauckham

The Reason for God
Timothy Keller

Titles from Dan

available on amazon.com

About the Author

Daniel P. Buttafuoco is a nationally recognized trial lawyer and apologist. He is the founding partner of the law firm Buttafuoco & Associates. In 1990, he wrote and graded the qualifying exam for the National Board of Trial Advocacy. He served as a church elder for 25 years and is the founder of the Historical Bible Society. He is also a noted speaker and author with over 8 million Internet views on Quora.

Over four decades in the courtroom have made him one of the most respected personal injury attorneys in the United States, with more than 100 jury and non-jury trials to his credit. He and his firm have secured over 175 separate settlements of $1 million or more for clients—including one of the three largest personal injury settlements in New York State history, and the single highest settlement ever for a police officer. His peers have consistently honored him as a "Super Lawyer," placing him among the top 5% of attorneys nationwide.

Dan combined his personal faith journey with his professional calling to law and theology. After earning his Master's degree in Theology, he dedicated himself to equipping believers to understand why they believe what they believe. Through the Historical Bible Society, he has preserved and shared ancient biblical texts and manuscripts, traveling nationwide to make Scripture accessible to both seekers and skeptics.

He is also the author of *Consider the Evidence: A Trial Lawyer Examines Eyewitness Testimony in Defense of the Reliability of the New Testament* and *5 Reasons Why the Bible is the Most Important Book You'll Ever Read.* With the same clarity, evidence, and care that have defined his legal career, Dan continues to defend the truth of the Bible and the faith it inspires.

Daniel P. Buttafuoco, Esq., B.A., J.D. & M.A. (Theology)

facebook.com/HistoricalBibleSociety

HistoricalBibleSociety.org